BIRDS AUSTRALIA

D0869637

Steve Parish Publishing Pty Ltd

A crimson rosella

BIRDS

Australia has over 750 species of birds, many of which are found nowhere else in the world. Some live on gibber plains and salt lakes, others in misty mountain rainforests; some are seabirds, others shorebirds, waterfowl or wildfowl. Each species is superbly adapted to its particular habitat.

For many of us, the power of flight is a miracle. As a bird's wings carry it high into the sky, our hearts soar in sympathy. There few things as beautiful as an eagle soaring, a gull hanging on the sea wind or the snowy wings of an egret carrying it across a billabong.

Birds can stir our sympathies in other ways as well. We laugh at parrots, with their brilliant colours and uninhibited antics; we marvel at the constructions of bowerbirds, and in the social interactions of birds such as crows and magpies we may see entertaining parallels with human affairs.

I look at birds and I am filled with wonder and delight. This little book contains images of a few of my feathered favourites.

• Hunters of the oceans •

The osprey (above) and the white-bellied sea-eagle (opposite) plunge into the sea to catch fish. The osprey may build its large stick nest in a seaside town, on a dead tree or even on a power pole.

• Long-legged ground birds •

The helmeted southern cassowary (left) and the bare-headed emu (opposite) have lost the power of flight, and move about on long, powerful legs. Males of both species sit on the eggs, then look after the striped chicks. The emu is common, but the cassowary is threatened by the destruction of the rainforests in which it lives.

• Superb songster •

A male superb lyrebird scratches up a display
mound and dances on it, his splendid tail cloaking
his body in shimmering silver. His loud song, which
includes mimicry of other birds, attracts females.

• The bigger they are •

This black-shouldered kite was on the alert for mice, and no threat to the willy wagtail, but the latter considered the tree home territory. With ferocious rattling cries, the pugnacious pygmy harassed the indifferent giant, until finally it flew away. Probably the kite just decided to shift, but the wagtail flirted its tail in triumph, sure the predator had fled in fear.

• Blue-cheeked charmers •

The crimson rosella is a gem of the Australian forests, its glowing scarlet, azure and sky-blue plumage lighting up the greens and browns of leaves and bark. Rosellas often visit seeding grasses and fruiting trees in small flocks, flirting and fanning their colourful cheek-patches and broad tails in sociable interactions.

• Choristers in evening dress •

Australia is the home of a black
and white brigade of birds
with outstanding choral talents.
The Australian magpie (left)
gathers in family parties and
carols to greet the dawn. The
pied butcherbird (right) has a
clear, ringing song which often
incorporates mimicry of other
birds' calls.

• The magnificent pelican •

The Australian pelican is a superb flier, which travels tremendous distances at high altitudes. It becomes tame at seaside resorts, but prefers to nest far inland on the shores of isolated salt lakes. Here chicks fledge in a race against time, for all too soon the shallow waters dry up and the fish on which the pelicans feed disappear.

• Living rays of sunshine •

The rainbow bee-eater (left) and eastern yellow robin (right) are familiar birds whose beauty never fails to astound. Bee-eaters are dazzling aerialists, taking dragonflies and wasps in flight. Robins lead more sedate lives, fossicking for insects on tree trunks and in foliage.

Over: Black-faced woodswallows

⋄ The hovering falcon ⋄

The nankeen kestrel is an
elegant small falcon which
hovers on slender wings over
roadsides and paddocks,
watching for grasshoppers and
mice. It may be seen anywhere
in Australia it can find prey
and a hollow in which to nest.
The kestrel at left is using a
termite mound as a perch; the
female opposite is sunning
herself on a ledge of Uluru.

• Seekers after sweetness •

High-pitched calls overhead call attention
to fast-flying lorikeets travelling from one
blossom-laden tree to another. The rainbow
lorikeet (opposite) and the scaly-breasted
lorikeet (above) are licking up nectar with
brush-tipped tongues.

• The all-Australian budgerigar •

When good rains fall Outback, budgerigars
pair up, find nest holes and produce chicks
until the native grasses stop seeding. These
enchanting parakeets are now kept by
fanciers world wide.

• Kings of the bushland •

Australian king-parrots are
seed- and fruit-eaters, which
are often seen in family parties
consisting of a brilliant male
(right), more sedately coloured
female (left) and several
youngsters. These gorgeous
parrots nest in hollows in trees
and readily come to garden
feeders.

• Kingfishers •

The forest kingfisher (left) belongs to a group which catches insects and small reptiles for food, and nests in holes in arboreal termite mounds. The azure kingfisher (right) is a more conventional feeder, darting into water to take small fishes, tadpoles or crustaceans. Its chicks are raised in a hole in a river bank.

• Laughing kookaburra •

The call of this giant kingfisher
resembles human laughter.

• Blue-winged kookaburra •

The call of this northern species
is raucous and maniacal.

• Two pigeons •

The introduced camphor laurel tree has helped the white-headed pigeon (right) become a common bird in coastal eastern Australia. The spinifex pigeon (left) lives in the harsh arid areas of inland Australia. Like all pigeons it must drink regularly and the best place to glimpse its crested elegance is at a desert waterhole.

• Spoonbills •

The yellow-billed spoonbill wades through shallow water, snapping up small creatures with its remarkable bill. Spoonbills are devoted mates and dedicated parents, who share nesting duties.

• Walking on lilies •

The comb-crested jacana has extremely long toes, which enable it to walk across the leaves of the lilies in the tropical wetlands where it lives. The male jacana incubates the eggs and looks after the chicks, tucking them under his wings to carry them away from danger.

◆ Growing up on a coral cay ◆

Birds which depend on the sea for a living,
like the red-tailed tropicbird (left) and black
noddy (above) find coral cays convenient
places to rear their chicks.

• Ducks, ducks, ducks •

Australia's wildfowl need all their powers
of flight to travel between wetlands as the
seasons change. The grey teal opposite is a
noted long-distance traveller. Above, a
family of Australian shelducks.

• Construction experts •

Male bowerbirds may build elaborate avenues and stages on which to sing and dance to attract females. This great bowerbird is carrying a decoration to his bower (above) and admiring the result (opposite).

• Waterbirds •

The eurasian coot (above) and dusky moorhen (right, with its chick) may be seen anywhere in Australia where there is fresh water. They are accomplished swimmers, which build their nests on islands and in reed clumps.

• Coloured like the rainforest •

Not all rainforest birds wear bright colours. The female satin bowerbird (left) does all the work of building the nest and rearing the chicks; her elegantly marked breast and green back blend with foliage and bark. The Lewin's honeyeater (opposite) spends its time in the canopy, delving into flowers in search of nectar. It wears the crescent "earring" typical of many Australian honeyeaters.

• Memories of home •

Early British visitors to Australia nostalgically named small scarlet-breasted birds "robins", although they were not related to the Old World robins. Above is a male scarlet robin and opposite the demure jacky winter.

• The cheerful cockatoos •

Australia is the land of parrots and cockatoos. Many are brightly coloured, but the yellow-tailed black-cockatoo (left) and sulphur-crested cockatoo (right) wear sombre black and dazzling white respectively, relieved by yellow on head and tail. While the sulphur-crest is comparatively common, many black-cockatoos are becoming increasingly rare.

◆ Aerial predators ◆

The hooked bills and large, keen eyes of these two birds identify them as predators. The wedge-tailed eagle (opposite) may take prey as large as small kangaroos, but is most often seen dining on a rabbit or a roadkill. The brown falcon (right) is a long-legged opportunist, as happy catching grasshoppers as picking up a small snake or lizard.

◆ Galahs galore ◆

The galah has benefited from
the cattle and sheep industries,
which provide watering points
in dry country, and from grain-
farming, which makes
available seed for galahs to eat.
These gorgeous parrots get
together after the nesting
season, forming flocks which
fill the skies with rose and
silver feathers as they circle
and swoop before descending
on a trough or waterhole.

• A graceful symbol •

The black swan is the State bird of Western
Australia and one of the world's best-known
waterfowl. These magnificent birds are
splendid parents to their downy cygnets.

• Night hunters •

The daytime portrait of the tawny frogmouth opposite shows its golden eyes. Its pupils will expand to make the eyes all-dark for hunting at night. The barn owl (right) has tip-tilted black eyes, and its keen sight is backed up by hearing which can locate a moving mouse in total darkness. Both frogmouth and owl have soft plumage which makes their flight nearly noiseless.

• Reef stalkers •

Egrets are long-legged, long-necked waterbirds, which stalk the shallows stabbing or snapping up fish and other water creatures. The eastern reef egret is unusual because it frequents salt water, feeding on the small life of coral or rocky reefs. Its chicks are reared in a nest built on a coral cay or island.

Steve Parish has recorded Australia, its wildlife and its people with his camera for many years. Steve's aim is to show people the marvels that exist in this long-isolated continent, with its unique cities, landscapes, plants and animals. His passion for Australia, and his awareness that urgent human action is needed to preserve its wildlife and places of beauty lends intensity to his superb photographs and evocative writing. Steve and his wife and partner Jan founded Steve Parish Publishing Pty Ltd to share with the world their vision of Australia.

Steve Parish
PUBLISHING

© Copyright photography and text Steve Parish Publishing Pty Ltd 1997
First published in Australia by Steve Parish Publishing Pty Ltd
PO Box 2160 Fortitude Valley BC Queensland 4006 Australia

Text: Pat Slater

PRINTED IN AUSTRALIA

ISBN 1 875932 69 0